I0388064

HIGHSCHOOL HORROR OFFICIAL MERCHANDISE

HSH©

HIGHSCHOOL HORROR OFFICIAL MERCHANDISE

HSH®

HIGHSCHOOL HORROR OFFICIAL MERCHANDISE

HSH©

HIGHSCHOOL HORROR OFFICIAL MERCHANDISE

HSH©

HIGHSCHOOL HORROR OFFICIAL MERCHANDISE

HSH

HIGHSCHOOL HORROR OFFICIAL MERCHANDISE

HSH©

HIGHSCHOOL HORROR OFFICIAL MERCHANDISE

HSH©

HIGHSCHOOL HORROR OFFICIAL MERCHANDISE

HSH©

HIGHSCHOOL HORROR OFFICIAL MERCHANDISE

HSH©

HIGHSCHOOL HORROR
OFFICIAL MERCHANDISE
HSH©

HIGHSCHOOL HORROR OFFICIAL MERCHANDISE

HSH©

HIGHSCHOOL HORROR OFFICIAL MERCHANDISE

HSH®

HIGHSCHOOL HORROR
OFFICIAL MERCHANDISE
HSH©

HIGHSCHOOL HORROR OFFICIAL MERCHANDISE

HSH©

HIGHSCHOOL HORROR OFFICIAL MERCHANDISE

HSH©

HIGHSCHOOL HORROR OFFICIAL MERCHANDISE

HSH©

HIGHSCHOOL HORROR OFFICIAL MERCHANDISE

HSH©

HIGHSCHOOL HORROR OFFICIAL MERCHANDISE

HSH©

HIGHSCHOOL HORROR OFFICIAL MERCHANDISE

HSH©

HIGHSCHOOL HORROR OFFICIAL MERCHANDISE

HSH®

HIGHSCHOOL HORROR OFFICIAL MERCHANDISE

HSH©

HIGHSCHOOL HORROR OFFICIAL MERCHANDISE

HSH©

HIGHSCHOOL HORROR OFFICIAL MERCHANDISE

HSH©

HIGHSCHOOL HORROR OFFICIAL MERCHANDISE

HSH©

HIGHSCHOOL HORROR
HSH©
OFFICIAL MERCHANDISE

HIGHSCHOOL HORROR OFFICIAL MERCHANDISE

HSH©

HIGHSCHOOL HORROR OFFICIAL MERCHANDISE

HSH©

HIGHSCHOOL HORROR OFFICIAL MERCHANDISE

HSH®

HIGHSCHOOL HORROR
OFFICIAL MERCHANDISE
HSH©

www.ingramcontent.com/pod-product-compliance
Lightning Source LLC
Chambersburg PA
CBHW081402080526
44588CB00016B/2570
* 9 7 8 1 9 1 4 0 7 1 3 6 2 *